CAREERS IN SEARCH AND RESCUE OPERATIONS

CAREERS IN THE

COAST GUARD'S

SEARCH AND RESCUE UNITS

Greg Roza

the rosen publishing group's

rosen
central

In Memory of William J. McConnell

Published in 2003 by The Rosen Publishing Group, Inc.
29 East 21st Street, New York, NY 10010

Library of Congress Cataloging-in-Publication Data

Roza, Greg.
Careers in the Coast Guard's search and rescue unit / Greg Roza.
    p. cm. — (Careers in search and rescue operations)
Summary: Discusses the history of the Coast Guard's Search and Rescue units, requirements of becoming a member of one of these units, and the role Guardsmen played after the events of September 11, 2001. Includes bibliographical references and index.
ISBN 0-8239-3835-2 (library binding)
1. United States. Coast Guard—Search and rescue operations—Juvenile literature. 2. United States. Coast Guard—Vocational guidance—Juvenile literature. [1. United States. Coast Guard—Vocational guidance. 2. Rescue work—Vocational guidance. 3. Vocational guidance.]
I. Title. II. Series.
VG53 .R69 2003
363.28'6—dc21

                                                                  2002013263

Manufactured in the United States of America

CONTENTS

INTRODUCTION

Semper Paratus

On the morning of September 11, 2001, two hijacked commercial airplanes crashed into the two towers of the World Trade Center in lower Manhattan. This event left many people feeling scared and vulnerable. Never before had terrorism of this magnitude reached American soil. As the day unfolded, U.S. armed forces sprang into action. Police officers, firefighters, emergency technicians, even construction workers and businesspeople rushed into the war zone to help however they could; tragically, many of those heroes lost their lives when the twin towers came crashing down. Despite the catastrophe that took place that morning, rescue workers demonstrated immense bravery, compassion, and skill.

Within minutes of the first attack, two Coast Guard helicopters stationed in Atlantic City, New Jersey, approached the scene, but they were unable to help because there was so much heavy smoke in the air. Two Coast Guard vessels from New York and New Jersey rushed in to evacuate the injured. They were soon joined by other Coast Guard ships, including a cutter (a small, fast ship) from Bayonne, New Jersey, and a buoy tender (a ship used to maintain buoys). The crew members on these ships rushed injured people to medical facilities that had been set up in Liberty State Park, New Jersey.

Throughout the day, the Coast Guard contributed to the rescue efforts in many other ways. A Coast Guard unit from Fort Dix, New Jersey, brought a mobile command post to the southern tip of Manhattan to aid the New York City Police Department. Another unit from Chesapeake, Virginia, flew a communications

In Nantucket, Massachusetts, four members of the U.S. Coast Guard return from a flight over the ocean after investigating the crash of an Egyptian airliner 60 miles (97 kilometers) offshore.

trailer in from Elizabeth City, North Carolina. The Coast Guard sent crew members, cutters, helicopters, and airplanes into the area to aid in the rescue mission. In addition, the Coast Guard called upon dozens of ships to help out, including an oil spill response vessel, ferries, tugboats, tour boats, cruise ships, and even privately owned boats. Between 10 AM on September 11 and 3 AM on September 12, the Coast Guard estimates that approximately one million people were evacuated from the southern tip of Manhattan.

The Coast Guard's participation did not end there. Before dawn on September 12, Coast Guard forces gathered in the waters around New York City and Washington, D.C., to secure ports. Helicopters from nearby cites were brought in to help transport people and supplies. Twelve Coast Guard cutters were soon on patrol in New York Harbor. Reservists and port security experts from as far away as St. Petersburg, Florida, were called in, and many others were put on alert. Coast Guard chaplains and stress management teams came to New York City to provide counseling for police officers, firefighters, and members of the armed forces. Coast Guard crews all over the United States patrolled and even shut down ports to ensure the safety of U.S. residents. Larger Coast Guard ships were positioned near major ports to protect the waterways. Despite all this activity, the Coast Guard continued to carry on with their day-to-day duties, which include patrolling for drug smugglers, protecting marine wildlife, and performing search and rescue missions.

On September 14, 2001, the U.S. Coast Guard cutter *Tahoma* tirelessly patrols New York Harbor. Even though it has been three days since the terrorist attacks on the World Trade Center, smoke still rises from the wreckage of the collapsed buildings.

Over the next few weeks, the Coast Guard continued to play a major role in cleaning up, providing protection, and preparing for a future that had become deeply uncertain. Two thousand Coast Guard reservists were activated on September 14 to help the regular Coast Guard do its job. Thirty-eight Coast Guard cutters were placed on patrol in New York Harbor. The Coast Guard heightened security in ports all over the nation, using cutters and aircraft to patrol the waters around them and carefully inspecting all incoming ships.

During its long history, the Coast Guard has developed into a diverse agency capable of responding to a variety of circumstances—large and small—with swift and precise action. For well over 100 years, the Coast Guard has used an ancient Latin phrase to describe the way they envision their job: *Semper Paratus*—"always ready."

No one is sure when this phrase became the Coast Guard's motto, but it was a Coast Guard captain named Francis Saltus Van Boskerck who penned the official Coast Guard anthem, "Semper Paratus," in 1922. Five years later, he wrote music to go with the words. Shortly after this, the phrase was added to the Coast Guard standard, or flag. Since then, the words of the anthem have been changed a little to reflect current times, but the new version remains true to the essence of Van Boskerck's original lyrics. The phrase Semper Paratus, the anthem based on that phrase, and the standard that bears those words have come to embody everything that the men and women of the Coast Guard value.

Coast Guard Anthem

"Semper Paratus"

Original words and music by Captain Francis Saltus
Van Boskerck, USCG
Copyright by Sam Fox Publishing Co., Inc.

From North and South and East and West,
The Coast Guard's in the fight.
Destroying subs and landing troops,
The Axis feels our might.
For we're the first invaders,
On every fighting field.
Afloat, ashore, on men and Spars,
You'll find the Coast Guard shield.

We're always ready for the call,
We place our trust in Thee.
Through howling gale and shot and shell,
To win our victory.
"Semper Paratus" is our guide,
Our pledge, our motto, too.
We're "Always Ready," do or die!
Aye! Coast Guard, we fight for you.

CHAPTER 1

Coast Guard History

The Coast Guard's past is an adventure story. It is inspiring, terrifying, and sometimes surprising. The fact of the matter is that the Coast Guard was originally part of the U.S. Treasury. The treasury controls our money—they make it, keep track of it, collect it during tax season, and enforce the federal laws regarding it. How does the Coast Guard fit in? It's an interesting story.

Early Origins

On January 14, 1784, the American Revolution ended. American citizens were no longer English colonists; they had earned their independence. The war, however, had left the infant country with very little money. The U.S. government was in need of funds to keep the new nation afloat. In order to raise money, Congress and the treasury of the United States taxed all goods coming into the United States from other countries. This was a desperate yet necessary move for the new government. British taxes had been one of the reasons that the colonists fought in the American Revolution, and few Americans wanted to pay taxes they thought were unfair.

During the war, many smugglers became heroes by outrunning British ships and sneaking goods into the colonies. After the war, these same smugglers were expected to pay tariffs on incoming goods. Most smugglers continued to sneak goods into the colonies. The leaders of the nation realized that something had to be done to enforce the new tariff laws.

President George Washington appointed Alexander Hamilton as the first secretary of the treasury. It was Hamilton's job to

The Coast Guard cutter *Manhattan*, built in 1872, patrols New York Harbor. It was transferred to the U.S. Navy after the start of the United States's involvement in World War II.

manage America's money. It was also his job to raise money for the country. Hamilton had to make some quick decisions regarding the smugglers and the lost revenue. He asked Congress for ten cutters to patrol the shores of the new nation and search for smugglers. He hoped to enforce the tariff laws and to raise more money for the United States.

On August 4, 1790, the Coast Guard was officially established, but it wasn't called the Coast Guard. This new agency was known by several names, including Reserve Cutters, Revenue Service, and Revenue Marine. The ten small cutters were required to patrol 2,000 miles (604 kilometers) of coastline. While there were probably people who thought Hamilton had wasted a little more than $10,000 by starting the Revenue Service, the brave, hardworking crews of the cutters did their best to prove them wrong. In the first ten years, the revenue that was collected on imports and exports rose from $52 million to $205 million.

Other Law Enforcement Duties

As the Revenue Service grew, they began to chase and apprehend pirates who preyed on honest (and dishonest) shipping companies. From 1794 until 1861 when the American Civil War began, the Coast Guard was responsible for preventing ships carrying African slaves from reaching the shores of the United States. During that time, the Coast Guard arrested many people who were involved in the foreign slave trade and freed about 500 slaves.

The Coast Guard has also been responsible for seizing illegal contraband. In 1920, Congress added the Eighteenth Amendment to the U.S. Constitution, which prohibited the manufacture, sale, transportation, import, and export of alcohol. During this time in American history (which became known as Prohibition), Coast Guard ships chased down and even sunk ships trying to bring alcohol into the United States. In recent years, the Coast Guard has focused its energies on drug smugglers trying to bring illegal drugs into the United States.

The Many Faces of the Coast Guard

The Coast Guard that we know today is a combination of several government agencies, each with a connection to maritime concerns. Through the years, these agencies were merged to form a single agency called the Coast Guard. In addition to law enforcement, the Coast Guard is also responsible for national defense, homeland security, protection of environmental resources, maritime search and rescue, freeing international and domestic waters from ice, maintaining navigational aids (lighthouses and buoys, for example), port security, and boating safety.

Lighthouses and Lightships

Before the Revenue Service was founded in 1790, there was a system of lighthouses and lightships (traveling lighthouses) in place to aid ships that were navigating at night and during stormy weather. In August 1789, America's new government created an agency to maintain lighthouses, buoys, and beacons that had been built by the colonies. This agency was called the Lighthouse Service.

Lighthouse keepers were often highly praised for their bravery. They had to stay at their stations for long periods of time, most often at night and during poor weather. Many women have served as lighthouse keepers since 1789. In fact, between 1828 and 1947, 138 women were employed as lighthouse keepers.

This lighthouse keeper uses binoculars to peer out over the Pacific Ocean from his perch in Big Sur, California. Without the help of lighthouses, the California coastline can be treacherous for ships trying to navigate at night.

Lightships have played a similar role in keeping American waters safe for ships. They kept watch in locations where it wasn't possible to build lighthouses. The first lightship patrolled the waters of Chesapeake Bay in 1820. Since then, there have been more than 120 lightships. Manning a lightship was a dangerous job. Many were sunk during storms or because of collisions with other ships. Today, lightships have been replaced by buoys that mark frequently traveled routes. However, lighthouses still play an important role in maritime safety and navigation.

Military

If you were to ask, most Coasties (as members of the Coast Guard are called) would probably say that as a branch of the military, the Coast Guard does not receive the same respect that the other branches receive. However, the Coast Guard has participated in nearly every American conflict since the United States became a country.

The Coast Guard is the oldest of the five branches of the U.S. military (Army, Navy, Air Force, Marines, and Coast Guard). The Continental navy, which had fought in the American Revolution, broke apart at the end of the war. Between 1790 and 1798, the Revenue Service was the only agency that protected American shores. The U.S. Navy was established in 1798 to help protect Americans at home and abroad. The Coast Guard continued to police the waters around America and protect American shores, but it also had a new responsibility: to aid the navy in times of war and at any other time that the president thought it necessary.

The first war in which the Coast Guard participated was a small war against French privateers in the Caribbean Sea from 1798 to 1799. It was the War of 1812, however, that helped to establish the Coast Guard's value as a military branch. Naval forces took advantage of the Coast Guard's small, quick cutters, which could outrun enemies close to the shore and along river routes. Since the War of 1812, the Coast Guard has fought in the Mexican War (1846–1848), the American Civil War (1861–1865), the Spanish-American War (1898–1899), World War I (1914–1918), World War II (1939–1945), the Korean War (1950–1953), the Vietnam War (1957–1975), and the Persian Gulf War (1990–1991).

In light of recent events, homeland security has become one of the most important responsibilities of the U.S. Coast Guard, perhaps even the most important. Historically, the Coast Guard has been protecting U.S. citizens since its earliest days. The people in the United States have been very fortunate; since the American Civil War, there has not been a major war fought on American soil. In part, the reason for this is because America is protected by two very large oceans. The U.S. military, and the Coast Guard specifically, have worked hard over the past 200 years to ensure against a foreign invasion by securing ports, patrolling waters, and investigating potentially threatening situations.

Environmental Protection

In 1822, Congress established a naval timber reserve (a forest where trees are grown to be used for building ships and other items). The Coast Guard was immediately placed in charge of protecting this reserve.

In 1867, the United States purchased Alaska from Russia. Seal hunting had become a problem in Alaska, and seals were in danger of extinction; approximately 250,000 seals were killed in the first four years after the United States purchased Alaska. In 1894, the Coast Guard set up a base in Alaska so that they could stop the illegal hunting of seals for their furs.

In 1885, the Coast Guard once again expanded their duties to include the protection of marine animals. The Coast Guard has enforced the laws regarding offshore fishing since that time. Since the early 1970s, the primary environmental duty of the Coast Guard has been combating pollution, especially oil spills.

Boating Safety and Inspection

Robert Fulton invented the steamboat in 1807. As steamboat travel grew more popular in the following years, boiler explosions became a serious problem. In 1837, a steamboat in North Carolina exploded, killing 100 people. This catastrophe prompted the federal government to create steamboat safety laws, and a new agency, the Steamboat Inspection Service, was entrusted with enforcing them. However, the laws were not that

Sinbad the Coast Guard Dog

One of the most famous Coast Guardsmen of all time wasn't human. Sinbad was a mutt adopted as the mascot of the Coast Guard cutter *Campbell* in 1937. Sinbad was a full-fledged member of the Coast Guard. He had his own bunk, his own specially made life preserver, and his own seat in the mess hall. He had even filled out his own enlistment papers (with a little help, of course).

During World War II, Sinbad crossed the equator several times, visited the Arctic, and crossed the international date line aboard the *Campbell*. The *Campbell* had been involved in numerous battles in the North Atlantic. By the end of the war, Sinbad had earned five ribbons of valor, just like the rest of the crew of the *Campbell*.

During his life, Sinbad "signed" autographs, was the subject of countless newspaper articles, appeared on television, and had a popular biography written about him titled *Sinbad of the Coast Guard*. Sinbad even starred in his own Hollywood movie in 1947, *Dog of the Seven Seas*.

In 1948, Sinbad retired from the *Campbell* and was assigned to the Coast Guard Lighthouse Station at Barnegat, New Jersey. There, he helped the crew watch for ships in danger. Sinbad passed away in 1951, after fifteen years as a dedicated member of the Coast Guard.

effective because no inspection standards were established, and each inspector used his own judgment on the safety of a steamship. As a result, in 1852, the Steamboat Inspection Act was passed, which helped to cut down on unsafe steamboats even though some problems still existed. Over the next fifty years, steamboat safety improved as safety regulations became even more strict and the Steamboat Inspection Service supplied their vessels with better fire fighting equipment.

The only Coast Guard member to be the subject of a biography, Sinbad (left) loyally served aboard the Coast Guard cutter *Campbell* for eleven

As recreational boating became popular, new laws were needed to fight the rising numbers of injuries and deaths that resulted from unsafe boating. In 1910, Congress passed the Motorboat Act, which made lights, whistles, fire extinguishers, and life preservers necessary boating equipment. In 1939, the Coast Guard Auxiliary was founded to further aid the regular Coast Guard in keeping boaters safe. Thanks to improved technology and stricter laws, the Coast Guard has effectively reduced the number of boating-related accidents.

Search and Rescue

The Coast Guard's search and rescue duties originated in 1831, when the secretary of the treasury authorized the use of one reserve cutter for the purpose of patrolling for ships and crews in danger. It wasn't until 1848, however, that a true lifesaving service began to come together. The government began to provide more effective equipment and storage facilities for search and rescue cutters. In 1871, the U.S. government officially funded the Life-Saving Service, which saved people from shipwrecks that occurred close to shore. More stations were built all along the East Coast of the United States, and new technology increased the success rate of lifesaving missions. Potential accidents were reduced because of improved navigational aids and better-constructed ships, but the drastic increase in the number of ships on the water made search and rescue missions crucial to maritime safety.

The twentieth century brought numerous innovations to search and rescue operations. Helicopters and amphibious aircraft (planes with floating devices that could land safely on water) made rescues quicker and more successful. The Coast Guard developed stations in the Atlantic Ocean and the Gulf of Mexico. Similarly, the Coast Guard developed a deepwater program with ships and aircraft that could operate for extended periods of time far out at sea. This allowed the Coast Guard to respond to distress calls far away from land. In the last thirty years, improved electronic equipment, computers, and communications technology have aided the Coast Guard in rescuing boaters in danger.

The Coast Guard Takes Shape

In 1915, the Revenue Service merged with the Life-Saving Service, forming a single agency called the Coast Guard that was responsible for patrolling U.S. waters and performing search and rescue missions. In the years following this merger, other agencies joined the Coast Guard, including the Lighthouse Service, the Steamboat Inspection Service, and the Bureau of Navigation.

Since 1967, the Coast Guard has been governed by the Department of Transportation in times of peace. In times of war, the Coast Guard is transferred to the Department of Defense. This demonstrates the flexibility that makes the United States Coast Guard a truly unique organization.

CHAPTER 2

The Coast Guard Today

Members of the Coast Guard have the chance to learn just about all there is to know about sailing and modern vessels. Similar to the other branches of the military, the Coast Guard is a great place to receive on-the-job training in a variety of professions: law enforcement, marine science, communications, electronics, and even food preparation and music. The Coast Guard offers more than just job training. When you enlist in any of the branches of the military, your first obligation is that of protecting your country. As with all U.S. military organizations, interested candidates must possess a strong desire to work hard and must be courageous when called upon.

Signing Up for the Coast Guard

Coast Guard boot camp is held in Cape May, New Jersey. Despite the fact that the Coast Guard is part of the Department of Transportation during times of peace, recruits can expect to take part in military training. Basic training usually lasts about eight weeks and involves hard physical exercise, classroom instruction, and specialized training sessions. Specialized training may include using ropes and tying knots, learning seamanship, and using a 9 mm handgun, for example. Once basic training is finished, new recruits are assigned to a station or ship. On-the-job training begins at this point. There is a wide range of jobs in the Coast Guard, from radar operator to law enforcement investigator, from marine science technician to weapons specialist.

Members of the Coast Guard are paid a monthly salary. New recruits make about $1,000 a month; newly commissioned officers make about $2,000. The salary depends on your level of experience and the amount of time you've been an enlisted member of the Coast Guard. While these numbers may seem somewhat low, enlisted individuals also receive generous benefits: yearly pay raises, free room and board, clothing expenditures, recreational allowances, free medical and dental care, retirement benefits, thirty days paid vacation every year, and college tuition for those who have been honorably discharged from the military.

Like the other branches of the military, you can learn more about the Coast Guard and basic training from your local recruiter. (Check the government listings in your local phone book to find the Coast Guard recruiter in your area.)

Coast Guard Academy

The Coast Guard Academy, located in New London, Connecticut, is a college for Coast Guard officers. Cadets who make it into the academy receive a full four-year scholarship and will earn a bachelor's degree in science by the time they finish. As in most colleges, the educational experience at the academy includes classroom training, athletics, internships, and leadership exercises. There are also music programs, a student government, and campus clubs. Upon graduation, each cadet becomes an ensign (the lowest rank

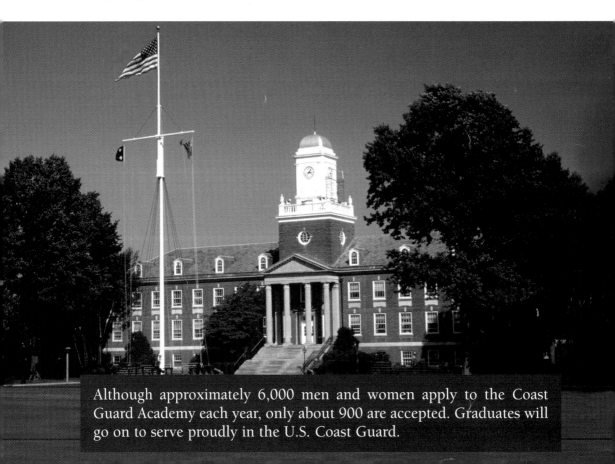

Although approximately 6,000 men and women apply to the Coast Guard Academy each year, only about 900 are accepted. Graduates will go on to serve proudly in the U.S. Coast Guard.

of commissioned officer) and is required to serve at least five years in the U.S. Coast Guard.

The majority of new cadets are in the top 25 percent of their graduating high school class. For those individuals willing to work hard and get good grades, it is one of the best ways to become an officer in the U.S. Coast Guard.

Coast Guard Reserves

The reserves are designed to enlarge the U.S. military forces in times of war. Reservists are required to attend training sessions one weekend a month and one week every year. When they are needed, reservists are called to active duty and join full-time members of the military in protecting the United States.

The Coast Guard Reserve was founded in 1941, after the United States joined World War II. Pay for new reservists is relatively low (about $130 for each weekend of training), but it increases the longer you are in the reserves and the higher your rank. The reserves also offer various benefits, such as signing bonuses and tuition packages. (To learn more about the Coast Guard Reserves, go to the URL listed on page 54.)

Coast Guard Auxiliary

The Coast Guard depends on volunteers to help educate citizens about boating laws and safety. This group of volunteers—

Coast Guard Ranks

    Seaman Recruit (boot camp)
    Seaman Apprentice (training and testing)
    Seaman
Noncommissioned Officers (NCOs)
    Petty Officer, 3rd Class
    Petty Officer, 2nd Class
    Petty Officer, 1st Class (may proceed to Commissioned Officer from here or continue in NCO ranks)
    Chief Petty Officer (CPO-1)
    Senior Chief Petty Officer (CPO-2)
    Master Chief Petty Officer (CPO3)
Commissioned Officers
    Chief Warrant Officer (CWO-1 through CWO-4)
Commissioned Officers from Academy or OCS (Officer Candidate School) Graduates
    Ensign (O-1)
    Lieutenant-JG (O-2)
    Lieutenant (O-3)
    Lieutenant Commander (O-4)
    Commander (O-5)
    Captain(O-6)
    Rear Admiral (O-7)
    Vice Admiral (O-8)
    Admiral (O-9)
    Admiral (O-10) (Commandant of U.S. Coast Guard)

approximately 33,000 of them—makes up the Coast Guard Auxiliary. After proper Coast Guard training, members of the Auxiliary can be called upon to help complete numerous tasks such as boating safety classes, navigational aid maintenance, safety examinations, radio watch at Coast Guard stations, recruiting, and search and rescue operations.

Women in the Coast Guard

Women have played important roles in the Coast Guard since its beginning, most notably as lighthouse keepers. On November 23, 1942, women were officially allowed to enlist in the U.S. Coast Guard as reservists. The U.S. government finally acknowledged that women had much to offer to the country as Coast Guardswomen. However, there were still obstacles for women to overcome at this point—female members of the Coast Guard could not serve overseas, for instance, and they could not issue orders to male members of the Coast Guard.

During World War II, many female members of the Coast Guard served their country as radar operators and LORAN (Long Range Aid to Navigation) technicians (for more information on LORAN, see page 34). After World War II, nearly all the women were phased out of the Coast Guard Reserves even though the other branches of the military continued to employ women.

It wasn't until 1973 that women were allowed to work side by side with men in the regular Coast Guard. This was also the year that the Coast Guard allowed women to become officers; the Coast Guard was the first branch of the military to do this. By 1978, all career fields within the Coast Guard—including positions on warships—were open to women. Today, women make up approximately 10 percent of the total members of the Coast Guard.

What Does the Coast Guard Do?

That's not an easy question to answer simply because the Coast Guard does so much. The Coast Guard has a long tradition of patrolling neighboring waters in order to enforce U.S. laws, especially laws relating to tariffs, to pirates, and to transporting contraband. Coast Guard law enforcement has extended to cover ship construction, boat inspections, pollution, the fishing industry, and the stopping of illegal aliens entering the country. Law enforcement, however, is only one aspect of Coast Guard activity. As the Coast Guard grew, so did its responsibilities.

Wartime Duties

The Coast Guard has two basic duties in times of war: to help the U.S. Navy by supplying it with men, women, and cutters; and to complete tasks with the skills specifically developed by the Coast Guard in times of peace, such as protecting America's coastlines.

In past wars, the Coast Guard has been used to patrol domestic waters, guard ports, capture or destroy enemy ships, escort and defend military and nonmilitary ships in foreign waters, and transport troops and equipment to locations all over the world. During World War II, Coast Guard ships sank a total of eleven Nazi submarines, including one that was rammed by the U.S. Coast Guard cutter *Campbell*.

Peacetime Duties

There are differences between the Coast Guard and the U.S. Army, Navy, Air Force, and Marines. Those branches of the military are exactly that—branches of the military. The Coast Guard, however, is a military organization with unique peacetime responsibilities. The sections that follow will address the peacetime duties of the Coast Guard.

Homeland Security

Homeland security—or the protection of people and property from hostile forces on U.S. soil—was thrust into the spotlight immediately after the tragic events of September 11, 2001. However, homeland security is not a new responsibility for the Coast Guard. The Coast Guard (or the agencies that would eventually become the Coast Guard) has protected the United States since the organization was founded.

The United States has more than 361 ports and about 95,000 miles (approximately 152,887 km) of coastline. It is a monumental task to protect these areas day in and day out. The Coast Guard works to keep transportation and commerce flowing smoothly while guarding U.S. borders against potential disasters. It is also responsible for making sure that the United States can quickly deploy military resources should the need arise. In essence, the Coast Guard is the first line of defense.

Boating Safety, Inspection, and Regulations

The Coast Guard regulates recreational boaters and boating areas similar to the way traffic officers regulate motorists and motorways. In 1971, Congress enacted the Federal Boat Safety Act to reduce the number of boating accidents that occur each year. In addition to providing safety instruction to recreational boaters, the Coast Guard also conducts inspections of private, passenger, and fishing vessels to make sure that they are safe to operate.

Since 1971, the number of recreational boats in U.S. waters has increased more than 100 percent, but the number of deaths resulting from boating accidents has fallen from 1,754 in 1971 to 701 in 2000. Despite the enormous improvement, the Coast Guard is still concerned; even one fatality is too many.

The Coast Guard Auxiliary conducts the Vessel Safety Check program. This is a free service provided by volunteer workers who check safety equipment on boats. They also supply boaters with information about the use of safety equipment.

The Coast Guard plays an important role in maintaining the safety of U.S. passenger ships. They oversee the design, construction, and operation of all passenger vessels. The Coast Guard also inspects fishing ships and trains their crews in safety procedures.

U.S. Coast Guard officers train in the San Francisco Bay in 2001. President George W. Bush's proposal to develop a Department of Homeland Security has changed the Coast Guard's role in the U.S. armed forces.

Environmental Protection

The Coast Guard helps to protect natural resources. Water pollution is an increasingly problematic issue, especially pollution resulting from oil spills. The Coast Guard does several things to prevent oil spills. They educate organizations and the crews of large oil tankers about the dangers of oil spills, enforce the laws pertaining to ships that carry large amounts of oil, and regularly inspect oil tankers to make sure that they are safe. In the instances when oil spills do occur, the Coast Guard has developed a rapid response cleanup team to combat environmental damage. These steps help the United States save billions of dollars a year.

Fishing is a significant U.S. business, and fishers run the risk of taking too many fish from U.S. waters. The Coast Guard enforces domestic and international fishery laws to ensure that we do not deplete our resources. They protect marine wildlife, such as seals and turtles, from hunters and natural predators. Foreign vessels are inspected before unloading to make sure that they do not contain species or bacteria that would be harmful to the native wildlife.

International Ice Patrol and Ice Breaking

In 1912, the RMS *Titanic*—the largest ocean liner ever built at the time—collided with an iceberg in the North Atlantic, resulting in the death of about 1,500 people. This event prompted countries on both sides of the Atlantic to gather to discuss safety in the transatlantic shipping lanes between Europe and North America. As of 1914, the U.S. Revenue Service, under orders from President Woodrow Wilson, established the International Ice Observation and Ice Patrol Service. Since then, the Coast Guard has used cutters and aircraft to patrol the Atlantic near Newfoundland in search of dangerous icebergs.

The headquarters for the International Ice Patrol Observation and Ice Patrol Service is located in Groton, Connecticut. The radar aircraft used for ice patrol are stationed in Elizabeth City, North Carolina. Since 1913, in the area monitored by the International Ice Observation and Ice Patrol, no lives or property have been lost as the result of iceberg collisions.

The Coast Guard is also responsible for keeping domestic and international shipping lanes free of ice with the help of ships called ice breakers. Ice breakers are large vessels that are strong enough to carve paths through shipping lanes blocked with ice. The Revenue Service began using ice breakers in 1867, when the United States purchased the state of Alaska from Russia. Since then, ice breakers have been used from San Francisco to Alaska, and from Chesapeake Bay to Greenland.

Aids to Navigation

It is the Coast Guard's job to make traveling in U.S. waters as easy and safe as possible. This means setting up and maintaining navigational aids. Today, there are 594 functioning lighthouses in the

United States. The Coast Guard also uses buoys, beacons, fog-horns, and weather forecasting to help ships find their way.

Modern technology has improved navigational aids. The first significant technological improvements in navigational aids were radio communication (invented in 1895) and tele-phones (invented in 1876). Two monumental navigational aids were developed during World War II: radar and LORAN. Radar is used to locate an object by bouncing radio waves off of it. LORAN is similar to but more accurate than radar. It also uses radio waves to pinpoint a specific location. Today, there are LORAN stations all over the world, and the Coast Guard uses them extensively. The Coast Guard also uses a technology called global positioning system, or GPS. GPS uses computers and satellites to determine an exact location on Earth.

Lifesaving

Of all the Coast Guard's responsibilities, perhaps none is more noble than search and rescue. Lifesaving missions are selfless struggles to ensure the safety of others while risking one's own life. Without Coast Guard search and rescue teams, recreational boaters, commercial shippers, fishery employees, and many others would have little or no hope of rescue after a disaster at sea. The next two chapters will take a closer look at the lifesaving responsi-bilities of the U.S. Coast Guard.

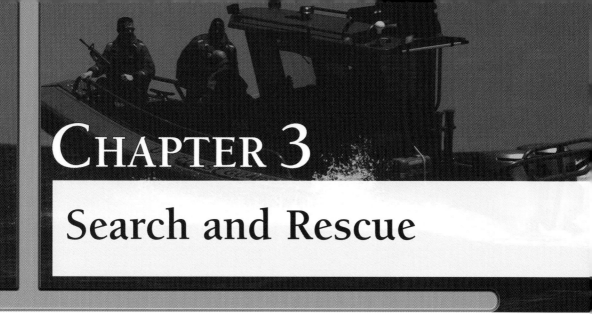

CHAPTER 3

Search and Rescue

At 3:35 AM, a call goes out at the search and rescue station: "Mayday! Mayday! Mayday! Our ship is going down!" As an officer listens to the call coming over the radio, a small crew of seamen rush to the 47-foot (14.3-meter) lifeboat prepared for this moment. They receive directions and speed out into a cold, rainy night. The waves are fierce, and the small vessel rocks dangerously as it rushes out to answer the distress call. Lightning flashes in the distance and sporadic fog banks obstruct the pilot's vision, but still they race on. Most experienced boaters would not be caught outside on a night like this, let alone on the water. The Coast Guard search and rescue team, however, won't let bad weather sway them from their sworn duty: to search out and rescue people in danger.

"So That Others May Live"

Search and rescue operations are one of the oldest functions of the U.S. Coast Guard. The original search and rescue agency, the Life-Saving Service, was founded in 1871, and it officially merged with the Revenue Service to form the Coast Guard in 1915. Since then, search and rescue units have continually sought ways to improve their success in rescuing people.

The first search and rescue vessels were small cutters propelled with oars, which, in many situations, were unable to rescue

The Coast Guard responds to a call about a downed pontoon plane near Washougal, Washington, on the Columbia River. Coast Guard divers search for the bodies of the plane's four passengers.

people on ships that had been torn apart by treacherous weather and turbulent coastal waters. Over the years, technical innovations helped to improve the Coast Guard's ability to save lives at sea. These innovations started with sturdier ships and rescue stations, and were followed by harpoonlike tools used to cast lines out to people and ships in danger, motorized vessels, powerful lights, radios, radar, amphibious airplanes and helicopters, and computers. Lifesaving techniques have also changed, as in the case of rescue swimmers.

One thing that has remained the same is that search and rescue teams put their lives on the line to save the lives of others. They rush into danger when there is no one else to do so. This trait is the basis for the motto uttered by search and rescue teams all over the world: "So that others may live."

Coast Guard Vessels

All boats (vessels under 65 feet [19.8 m] in length) and cutters (those over 65 feet [19.8 m]) may be used for search and rescue missions. These include swift motorboats, buoy tenders, law enforcement patrol boats, ice breakers, tugboats, and large, high-endurance cutters. Small, fast, and powerful surfboats are needed to rescue people who are trapped in rough waters close to shore. The small boats allow the Coast Guard to get in and get out quickly. An ice breaker might be needed to reach people in Arctic or wintry environments. Large cutters may be used for deepwater rescue missions.

Aircraft and Helicopters

Aircraft and helicopters also play important roles in the day-to-day affairs of search and rescue operations. Such aircraft can often reach a vessel in distress faster than a cutter or motorboat. Amphibious planes can land on water near vessels in danger and take people to safety. Jets can travel long distances in a short amount of time.

The helicopter was developed by the Coast Guard during World War II to combat submarines. Later, the helicopter was worked into the search and rescue program. Helicopters, armed and unarmed, can travel long distances in a short amount of time and are vital in rescuing boaters from perilous conditions. A helicopter can hover over a specified area, lower a rescuer into the water, pluck a drowning person from the water, and rush injured boaters to medical facilities miles away.

Modern Technology

Technological advances have also allowed the Coast Guard to improve their ability to rescue people. Computers, communications systems, radar, LORAN, and GPS all play important roles in locating boaters in danger. At the time of the publication of this book, the Coast Guard is in the process of updating its fleet of vessels and aircraft, many of which are thirty and forty years old. New and improved ships will increase the Coast Guard's ability to respond quickly during search and rescue missions. The newest rescue vessel is a 47-foot (14.3-meter) motor lifeboat that is faster and sturdier than older Coast Guard vessels. In addition, it can withstand near-hurricane gusts, navigate 20-foot (6-meter) waves, and can right itself if it tips over during stormy weather.

The Canadian Coast Guard's fleet of icebreakers keeps ship routes open when the northern coastal waters freeze. An icebreaker's control room, pictured here, is equipped with sophisticated radar and computer technology.

Rescue Swimmers

The helicopter made rescuing capsized boaters quicker and easier than it had ever been before. A basket could be lowered to someone in danger, and that person could be raised to safety in very little time. However, there were still problems that needed to be solved. Rough waters make it impossible for amphibious helicopters to land. Also, the colder the water, the

The U.S. Coast Guard uses helicopters to rescue people who are stranded in the ocean. In Seattle's Puget Sound, a Coast Guard helicopter and its crew practice doing just that.

less time victims have until hypothermia (low body temperature) sets in. Hypothermia greatly reduces the time available for rescue because it depletes a person's strength, numbs their limbs, and renders them unconscious.

In 1982, a ship named the *Marine Electric* sank off the coast of Virginia. The Coast Guard was quick to respond, but the waters were rough and freezing cold, and it was nearly impossible to help the thirty-four crew members who quickly succumbed to hypothermia. Helicopters lowered rescue baskets, but the men were too cold and tired to climb into them. Thirty-one members of the crew perished in the icy waters.

This tragedy may have been avoided if a rescue swimmer had been present that day. A rescue swimmer—wearing a thermal suit and swim fins—can be lowered into the cold water to help people into rescue baskets. Nine years after the *Marine Electric* tragedy, rescue swimmers became a part of every Coast Guard air station. By January 2001, Coast Guard rescue swimmers had saved more than 4,000 people.

CHAPTER 4

True Stories

Search and rescue is a complex job, one that can be calm one day and turbulent the next, or fulfilling one day and tragically sad the next. Only true stories of Coast Guard search and rescue can appropriately convey the intricate nuances of this demanding yet rewarding profession.

Terror on the Ice

The following true story was described in the book *Lifeboat Sailors* by retired Coast Guard senior chief Dennis L. Noble.

On February 10, 1996, Petty Officer Jeffery Kihlmire was stationed in Charlevoix, Michigan. That evening, freezing rain turned to snow and high winds by nightfall. Kihlmire's station soon got a call from someone who had heard a desperate voice calling for help out on the ice of Lake Michigan. Kihlmire and his crew arrived at the shore shortly after 8:00 PM. They could barely make out a person about 200 yards out on the lake. It was a man who had been driving a snowmobile in the snowstorm and had lost his way. He had drifted out onto the lake and fell through a patch of thin ice. Now he clung to the ice as he screamed for help. Hypothermia was setting in, and his strength was failing. Kihlmire had to act quickly.

Kihlmire put on a wet suit, a life jacket, and a special harness attached to a line that other crew members secured on shore. In the icy wind and stinging snow, Kihlmire crawled out on the ice, holding a flashlight in his mouth. His limbs frequently broke through the ice as he crawled. Finally, he reached the nearly unconscious man. Several other Coast Guard personnel had crawled out after Kihlmire, and together they slowly dragged the man toward the

Pack ice on the surface of the Detroit River obstructs the path of this cargo ship, which is on its way to the lower Great Lakes. A U.S. Coast Guard tugboat lends a helping hand, pulling the ship to its destination.

shore. The ice around them kept breaking, and the icy waters nearly dragged them down. They reached thicker ice and worked the victim into a sled that they had brought out to him. Back on shore, they raced the man to a waiting ambulance.

The whole ordeal had taken about fifteen minutes. Thanks to the quick actions of Petty Officer Kihlmire and his crew, the man was saved. Unfortunately, they realized too late that the man's brother had also crashed through the ice. They went back and searched for him, but he was never found.

This story exemplifies the wide range of duties and emotions associated with many search and rescue operations. Kihlmire and his crew rushed back into a perilous situation when they realized that there had been a second man, despite the fact that they knew he probably could not be saved. While Kihlmire and his crew were rewarded for their bravery, a life was lost to the waters that stormy night.

A Perilous Rescue

This true story is based on an article that first appeared in *People* magazine on July 31, 2000.

On October 30, 1991, rescue swimmer David Moore joined his crewmates for a dangerous rescue mission 60 miles (96.6 km) south of Martha's Vineyard, Massachusetts. A massive storm had hit the area, and a small sailboat called the *Satori* was in danger of being destroyed by monstrous waves, some nearly 80 feet (24.4 m) high. At first, the helicopter crew was sent as a precaution, since a Coast Guard cutter, the *Tamaroa*, was on-site to make the rescue. The crew members from the Coast Guard cutter were soon in danger of drowning, and David Moore was forced to jump into action.

Moore dived into the churning waters below the helicopter. He immediately felt lost among the towering waves. It was so bad that Moore needed to go back up to the helicopter to try another dive. The second time he landed closer to the *Satori* and the three members of its panicked crew. He struggled until he had all three safely in the helicopter. Moore then dived back into the turbulent waters a third time to rescue the crew of the *Tamaroa*.

The Coast Guard rescuers were not finished, however. There were other guardspeople in danger. Another Coast Guard helicopter went down just 15 miles (24 km) from where the *Satori* rescue had occurred, leaving its crew to be tossed about by waves 70 to 80 feet (21 to 24 m) tall. The battered crew was miraculously saved by a third helicopter rescue team that had been in the area. The crew of the *Tamaroa* went on to save another boater, despite being rescued themselves just hours before. Tragically, one member of the crew died in the violent storm and was never recovered.

On this day, members of the Coast Guard were called upon to rescue both civilian and Coast Guard personnel. Considering the chaotic weather conditions, it was remarkable that only one person was lost to the storm. This event was related in a 1977 book and a film in 2000, both called *The Perfect Storm*.

CHAPTER 5

How September 11, 2001, Changed the Coast Guard

Immediately after the attack on the World Trade Center, it was obvious to U.S. leaders that security measures would have to change, and that it would take the cooperation of numerous agencies and individuals. How would the Coast Guard and the other branches of the armed forces respond to the tragic events of 9/11? What changes would have to be made in order to ensure the safety of millions of people? Those were questions that had to be considered and answered quickly.

Changes were made, and quickly. As a first line of defense, the Coast Guard was expected to make many of these changes. U.S. ports are very important to the U.S. economy because of the large volume of people, ships, and packages that pass through them every day. In light of this, it is probably obvious that most of the changes the Coast Guard made were related to keeping U.S. ports safe.

In the days following the World Trade Center attack, more than 50 percent of the Coast Guard's budget was used for port security, compared to the 2 percent given to port security before September 11, 2001. As of September 14, 2001, no nonmilitary vessels may come within 100 yards (91.4 m) of U.S. Navy ships unless they first receive permission. To enforce these rules, the Coast Guard patrols the safety zones around navy ships. Other security zones were set up around power plants, marine services, and hazardous freight vessels. The Coast Guard also extended the advance notice a vessel must give before entering a U.S. port from twenty hours to ninety-six hours. This gives the Coast Guard more time to investigate the vessel.

The *Svesdu-Maru*, a 152-foot (30-m) boat, was carrying an illegal cargo—cocaine. This Coast Guard officer stands next to over 13 tons (11.28 metric tons) of the drug—the largest maritime cocaine seizure of all time.

U.S. Coast Guard Core Values

In 1994, the Coast Guard Academy established core values for their officers. These core values have become a very important aspect of training new officers. They have also become guiding principles for all Coast Guard personnel. Since 1998, Coast Guard Academy cadets are evaluated in part according to the three Coast Guard core values. The following is the official Coast Guard report regarding their core values:

Honor: Integrity is our standard. We demonstrate uncompromising ethical conduct and moral behavior in all of our personal actions. We are loyal and accountable to the public trust.

Respect: We value our diverse work force. We treat each other with fairness, dignity, and compassion. We encourage creativity through empowerment. We work as a team.

Devotion to Duty: We are professionals, military and civilian, who seek responsibility, accept accountability, and are committed to the successful achievement of our organizational goals. We exist to serve. We serve with pride.

Several key issues soon came to the forefront as matters that are vital to homeland security. Boating safety was another important issue. Improved boating safety means less time spent on search and rescue missions and more time to protect navy ships and ports. The Coast Guard wanted to improve communication between its divisions, and between itself and federal, state, and local agencies, as well as civilian boaters. The Coast Guard wanted to improve the transportation system so that people could get the most out of the U.S. waterways while providing the most protection; this could include anything from implementing the use of tamper-proof containers for shipping to improving the control of high-priority ships, such as oil tankers and cruise ships. Equipment and vessels needed to be updated.

During Operation Desert Storm, the U.S. Coast Guard provided valuable security escorts to allied ships traveling through the Middle East. This motorboat guards the cargo ship *Pfc. Dewayne T. Williams* in Saudi Arabia.

Technology and information systems needed to be modernized. Training needed to be redesigned to ensure that members of the Coast Guard were properly prepared for modern dilemmas. The Coast Guard needed to concentrate on developing the deep-water project to improve their ability to respond to unforeseen dangers. On top of all these changes, the Coast Guard also vowed to stay dedicated to all of their duties, from search and rescue to environmental protection.

Is this a difficult mission? Absolutely, but the Coast Guard is up to it. They have always been responsible for adapting to new dangers and for solving new problems. In the years to come, the Coast Guard will continue to evolve as America's needs arise, and Coast Guard members will always be prepared to risk their lives while protecting American citizens and property. Whether they are called upon to protect ports, to go overseas to assist the U.S. Navy, or to perform vital search and rescue missions close to home, the U.S. Coast Guard will stand by their motto: Semper Paratus—always ready.

GLOSSARY

amphibious Able to function on land or in air and in water.

anthem A song celebrating the greatness of a country or an organization.

beacon A powerful light or horn used to guide vessels near coastal areas.

buoy A floating object anchored in shallow waters that marks a safe path for vessels.

cadet A student at a military school who is training to be an officer.

contraband Goods that are illegal to import, export, and possess.

cutter A small, fast Coast Guard ship designed to "cut" through waves.

hypothermia Dangerously low body temperature.

lightship A ship with a powerful light, used in place of a lighthouse.

maritime Of or relating to the sea.

Mayday An international radio and telephone word used as a distress signal.

navigation The act of planning a course for a ship or an aircraft.

radar The method of detecting distant objects by analyzing radio waves reflected from their surfaces.

recruit A new member of a military force.

smuggle To secretly and unlawfully import or export goods without paying the taxes normally placed on those goods.

standard A flag or banner, especially that of a military force.

tariff A fee or list of fees imposed by a government on imported and exported goods.

terrorism The unlawful use of force or violence to intimidate societies or governments, often for ideological reasons.

vessel A ship, usually larger than a rowboat.

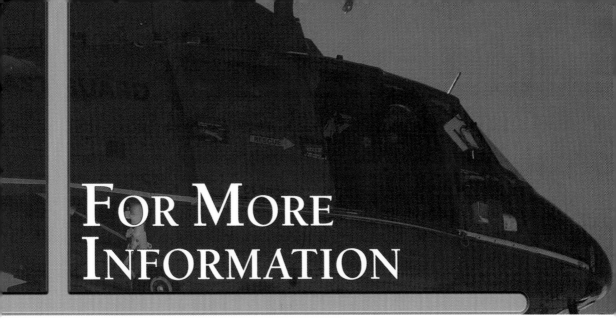

FOR MORE INFORMATION

The American Legion
National Headquarters
Indianapolis Office
700 North Pennsylvania Street
P.O. Box 1055
Indianapolis, IN 46206
(317) 630-1200
Web site: http://www.legion.org

The National Association for Uniformed Services
5535 Hempstead Way
Springfield, VA 22151
(703) 750-1342
Web site: http://www.naus.org

United Armed Forces Association
P.O. Box 20672
Waco, TX 76702
(888) 457-7667
Web site: http://www.uafa.org

Women Officers Professional Association
WOPA
P.O. Box 1621
Arlington, VA 22210
Web site: http://www.wopa.org

Web Sites

Due to the changing nature of Internet links, the Rosen Publishing Group, Inc., has developed an online list of Web sites related to the subject of this book. This site is updated regularly. Please use this link to access the list:

http://www.rosenlinks.com/csro/cgsr/

FOR FURTHER READING

Canney, Donald L. *U.S. Coast Guard and Revenue Cutters, 1790–1935*. Annapolis, MD: Naval Institute Press, 1995.

Department of Defense. *21st Century Complete Guide to the U.S. Coast Guard: Current Events, News, Homeland Security, Immigration, Vessels, Aircraft, Lighthouses, Polar Icebreaking, History, At War, and Safety*. CD-ROM. Progressive Management, 2002.

Johnson, Robert Erwin. *Guardians of the Sea: History of the United States Coast Guard, 1915 to the Present*. Annapolis, MD: Naval Institute Press, 1988.

Larzelere, Alex, and Brent Scowcroft. *The Coast Guard at War: Vietnam, 1965–1975*. Annapolis, MD: Naval Institute Press, 1997.

Noble, Dennis L. *That Others Might Live: The U.S. Life-Saving Service, 1878–1915*. Annapolis, MD: Naval Institute Press, 1994.

Shanks, Ralph C., Wick York, and Lisa Woo Shanks, ed. *The U.S. Life-Saving Service: Heroes, Rescues, and Architecture of the Early Coast Guard*. Petaluma, CA: Costāno Books, 1996.

Stonehouse, Frederick. *Lighthouse Keepers & Coast Guard Cutters: Heroic Lighthouse Keepers and the Coast Guard Cutters Named After Them*. Gwinn, MI: Avery Color Studios, Inc., 2000.

BIBLIOGRAPHY

American Maritime Congress. "After 9/11: Maritime News Following the Tragedy." Retrieved March 25, 2002 (http://www.us-flag.org/af911marnewf.html).

Carney, James C. "U.S. Coast Guard: The 'Forgotten' Military." 2001. Retrieved May 15, 2002 (http://www.jacksjoint.com/the_forgotten_military.htm).

Ferrell, Nancy Warren. *The U.S. Coast Guard*. Minneapolis, MN: Lerner Publications, 1989.

Grunts.net. "United States Coast Guard: Search and Rescue." Retrieved May 16, 2002 (http://www.grunts.net/uscg/sar.html).

Hamilton, Robert A. TheDay.com. "New Methods of Protecting Ports Needed: Coast Guard Expert Says Terrorist Targets Are Many." February 7, 2002. Retrieved March 25, 2002 (http://www.theday.com/news/sp-report3.asp?NewsUID=0A2822B4-9D6C-4551-8B65-6EB11C4BA3D4&rec=9).

Herbert, James W. "U.S. Coast Guard Ranks." 1996. Retrieved
May 16, 2002 (http://continuouswave.com/boats/bristolBay/
rank.html).

Korb, Lawrence J. Council on Foreign Relations. "Meeting
Summary. Homeland Security: A Coast Guard Perspective."
2001. Retrieved June 4, 2002 (http://www.cfr.org/public/
resource.cgi?pub!4355).

Krietemeyer, Captain George E. *The Coast Guardsman's
Manual*. Annapolis, MD: Naval Institute Press, 2000.

Noble, Dennis L. "A Legacy: The United States Life-Saving
Service." November 2001. Retrieved May 15, 2002
(http://www.uscg.mil/hq/g-cp/history/h_USLSS.html).

Noble, Dennis L. *Lifeboat Sailors*. Washington, DC:
Brassey's, 2000.

Scheina, Robert. "The Coast Guard at War." January 1999.
Retrieved May 15, 2002 (http://www.uscg.mil/hq/g-cp/
history/h_Cgatwar.html).

Scheina, Robert. "U.S Coast Guard: A Historical Overview."
January 1999. Retrieved May 15, 2002 (http://www.uscg.mil/
hq/g-cp/history/h_USCGhistory.html).

Snyder, John. "Ferries to the Rescue After World Trade Center
Terror Attack." October 2001. Retrieved June 4, 2002
(http://www.marinelog.com/DOCS/PRINT/mmiocfer1.html).

TheDay.com. "Securing the Border." February 16, 2002.
Retrieved March 25, 2002 (http://www.theday.com/news/

sp-report3.asp?NewsUID=B888C9E4-B087-426D-9206-CCA06078C812&rec=9).

United States Coast Guard. "A Brief History of the Coast Guard Reserve." June 1995. Retrieved May 15, 2002 (http://www.uscg.mil/hq/reserve/reshist.htm).

United States Coast Guard. "The Coast Guard & Homeland Security." January 2002. Retrieved May 15, 2002 (http://www.uscg.mil/hq/g-cp/history/Homeland_Security.html).

United States Coast Guard. "Coast Guard Rescue Swimmers." January 2002. Retrieved May 15, 2002 (http://www.uscg.mil/hq/g-cp/history/Rescue_Swimmer_History.html).

United States Coast Guard. "Deepwater Roles & Missions." Retrieved May 29, 2002 (http://www.uscg.mil/hq/g-a/Deepwater/MISSIONS/Missions%20Assets%20History.htm).

United States Coast Guard. "Enlisted Rating Guide." January 2001. Retrieved May 15, 2002 (http://www.uscg.mil/overview/InsigniaCombined14.jpg).

United States Coast Guard. "The Essence of the Coast Guard: America's Maritime Guardians." Retrieved May 15, 2002 (http://www.uscg.mil/overview/essence_of_the_coast_guard.htm).

United States Coast Guard. "Homeland Security." March 2002. Retrieved May 29, 2002 (http://www.uscg.mil/hq/g-a/Deepwater/MISSIONS/threats.htm).

United States Coast Guard. "International Ice Patrol History." Retrieved May 29, 2002 (http://www.uscg.mil/lantarea/ iip/iiphist.html).

United States Coast Guard. "International Ice Patrol Mission." Retrieved May 29, 2002 (http://www.uscg.mil/lantarea/iip/ iipmis.html).

United States Coast Guard. "New Rules to Fight Terrorism Announced." May 28, 2002. Retrieved May 29, 2002 (http://www.uscg.mil/d5/news/2002/r052_02.html).

United States Coast Guard. "Recreational Boating Safety." Retrieved May 30, 2002 (http://www.uscg.mil/overview/ issue%20rbs.htm).

United States Coast Guard. "Sinbad, USCG (Ret.): K9C (Chief Petty Officer, Dog)." October 2001. Retrieved March 15, 2002 (http://www.uscg.mil/hq/g%2Dcp/history/faqs/sinbad.html).

United States Coast Guard. "U.S. Coast Guard Core Values." Retrieved May 16, 2002 (http://www.uscg.mil/hq/g%2Dw/ g%2Dwt/g%2Dwtl/values.htm).

United States Coast Guard: Office of Boating Safety. "Tips for Preventing Boating Injuries and Fatalities." Retrieved May 30, 2002 (http://www.uscgboating.org/saf/saf_yrdeathgraph.asp).

United States Coast Guard Academy. "Academy History and General Information." July 1998. Retrieved May 15, 2002 (http://www.cga.edu/history.html).

The Wheelhouse Report. "The Coast Guard Responds to the Terrorist Attacks." Retrieved June 4, 2002 (http://www.wheelhousereport.org/to/cg/cgresp.html).

INDEX

About the Author

Greg Roza is a children's book editor and a freelance author living in upstate New York with his wife, Abigail, and their daughter, Autumn.

Photo Credits

Cover, pp. 5, 19, 40, 47, 49 © Corbis; p. 1 © Brandon Brewer/AP/Wide World Photos; p. 7 © Scott Carr/AP/Wide World Photos; p. 11 © U.S. Coast Guard; p. 14 © Chris Rainier/Corbis; p. 24 © Todd Gipstein/Corbis; p. 31 © AP/Wide World Photos; p. 36 © Jeremiah Coughlan/AP/Wide World Photos; p. 39 © Bojan Breceli/Corbis; p. 43 © James L. Amos/Corbis.

Editor

Annie Sommers

Designer

Nelson Sá